Old Mister Rabbit

An African American Folk Song
Illustrated by Robert Bender

for little Briana

HARCOURT BRACE & COMPANY
Orlando Atlanta Austin Boston San Francisco Chicago Dallas New York
Toronto London

4

Old Mister Rabbit,
You've got a mighty habit
Of jumping in my garden

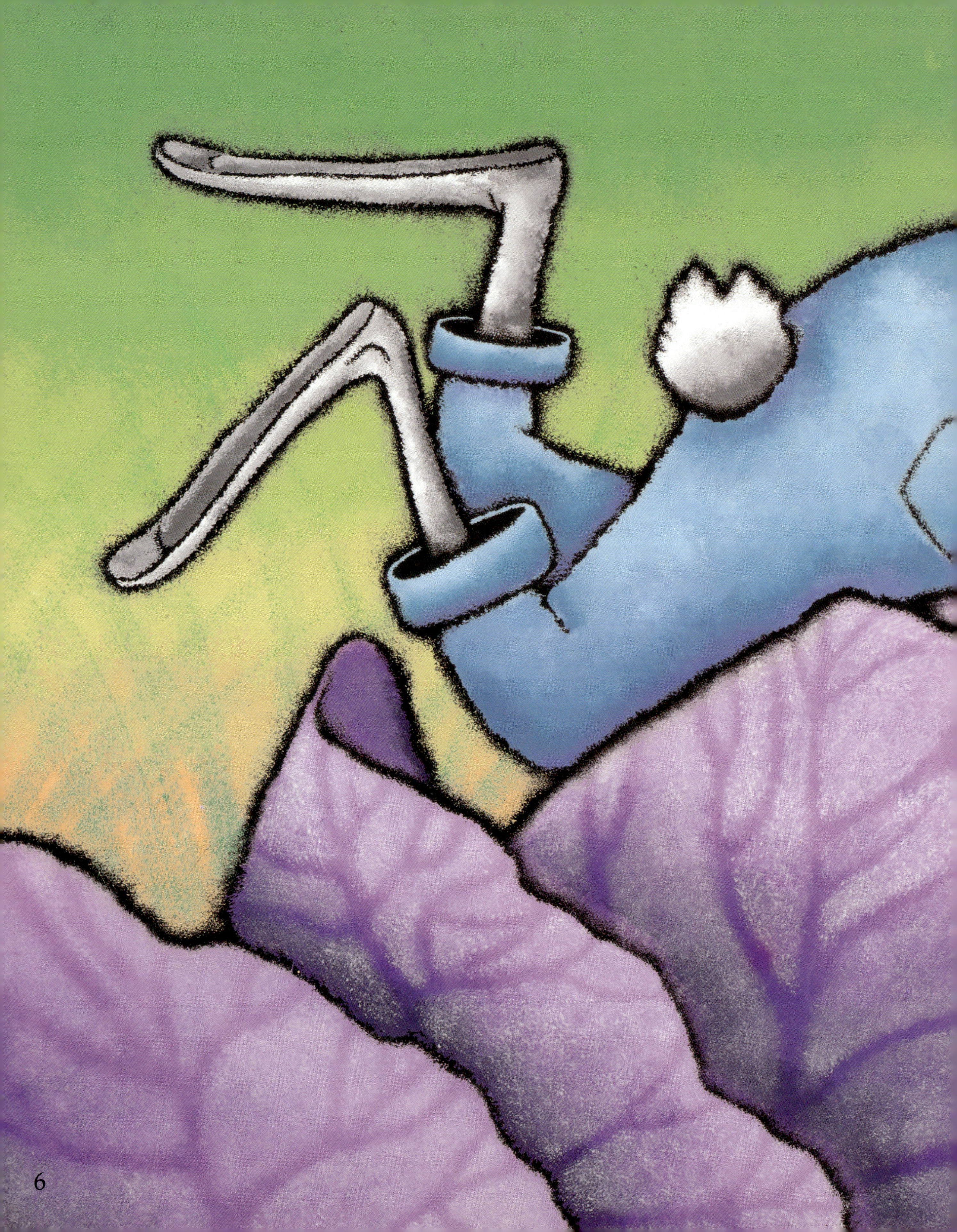

And eating all my cabbage.

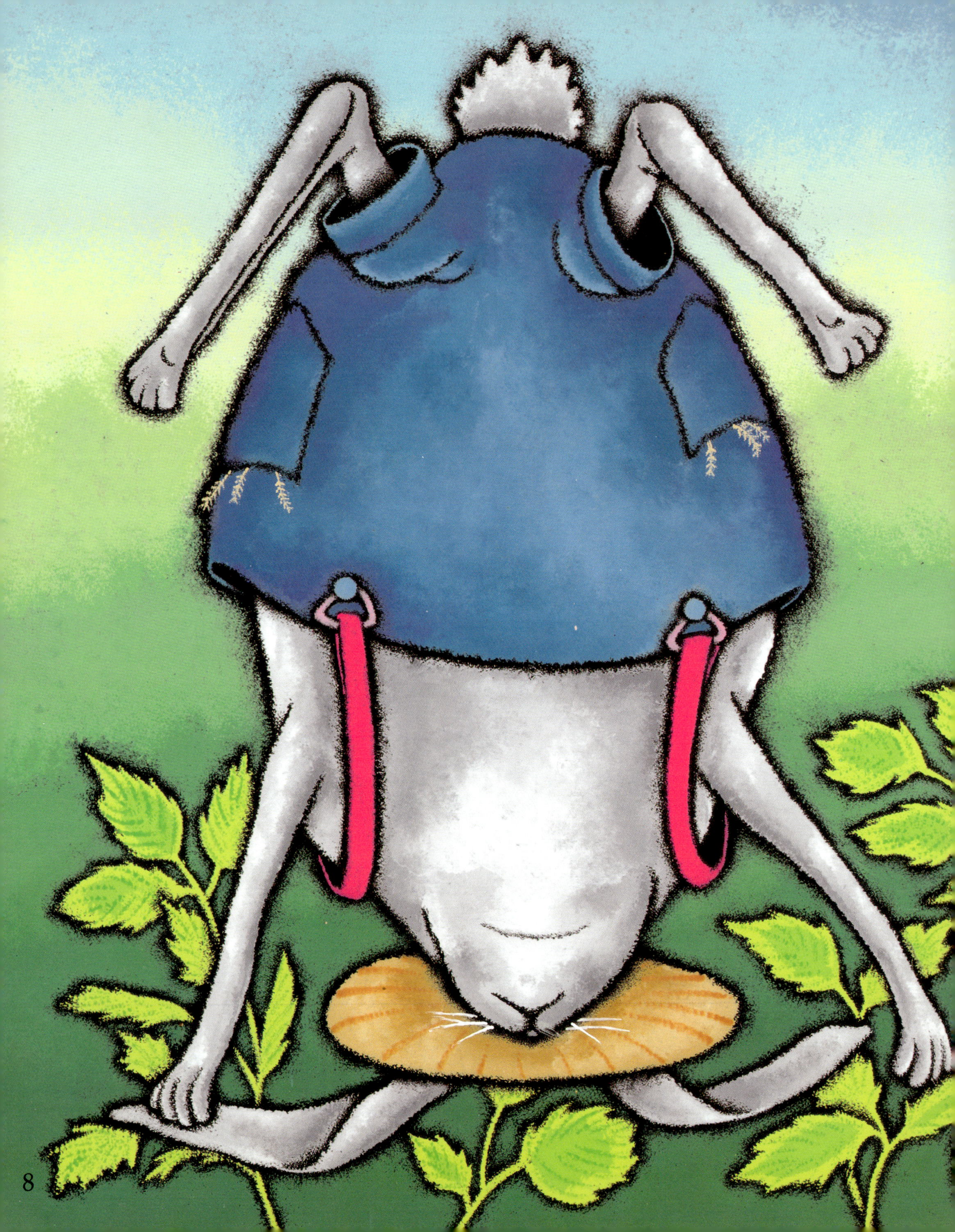

Old Mister Rabbit,
You've got a mighty habit,
Of jumping in my garden

10

And eating all my tomatoes.

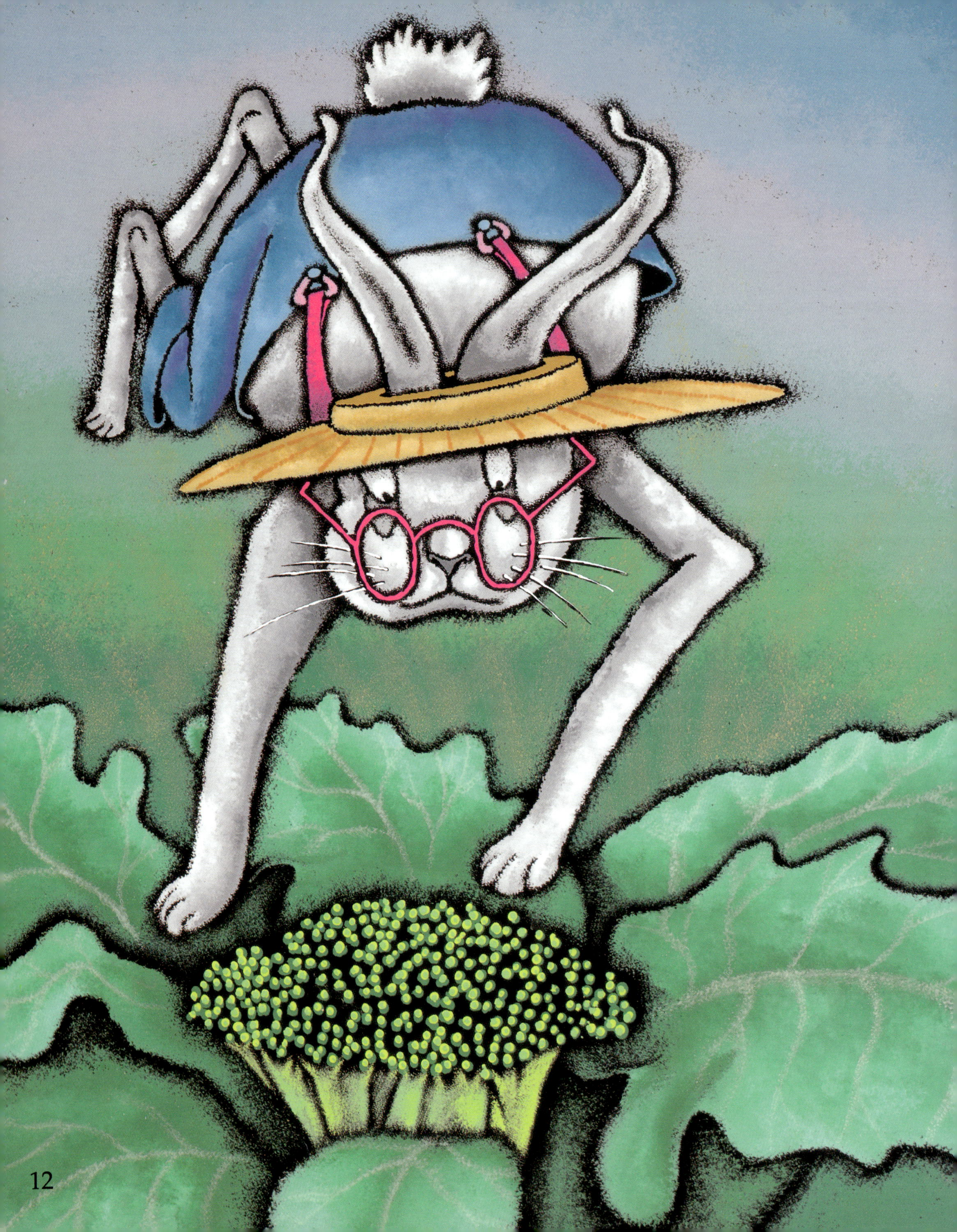

Old Mister Rabbit,
You've got a mighty habit
Of jumping in my garden

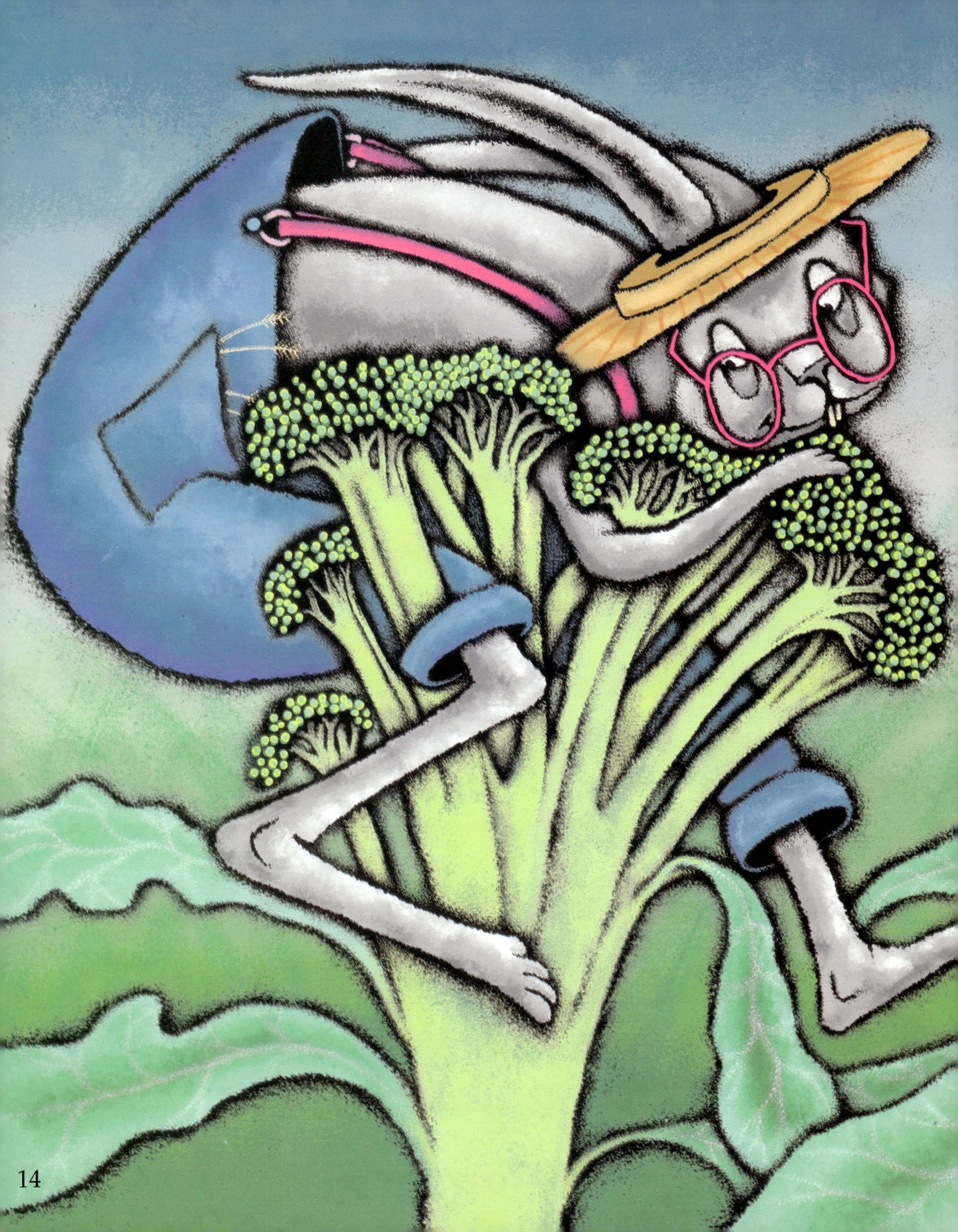

And eating all my broccoli.

16

Old Mister Rabbit,
You've got a mighty habit
Of jumping in my freezer

18

And eating all my ice cream!

20

21

Old Mis- ter Rab - bit, you've got a might - y hab - it,

Of jump- ing in my gar - den and eat - ing all my cab - bage.

Illustrations copyright © by Harcourt Brace & Company

All rights reserved. No part of this publication may be reproduced
or transmitted in any form or by any means, electronic or
mechanical, including photocopy, recording, or any information storage
and retrieval system, without permission in writing from the publisher.

Requests for permission to make copies of any part of the work
should be mailed to: Permissions Department, Harcourt Brace & Company,
6277 Sea Harbor Drive, Orlando, Florida 32887-6777.

HARCOURT BRACE and Quill Design is a registered trademark of
Harcourt Brace & Company.

Grateful acknowledgment is made to Michael Seeger,
on behalf of the family of Ruth Crawford Seeger,
for permission to reprint the music
from "Old Mister Rabbit" in *American Folk Songs
for Children* by Ruth Crawford Seeger.
Music copyright 1948 by Ruth Crawford Seeger.
Published by Doubleday (still in print).

Printed in the United States of America

ISBN 0-15-307286-5

4 5 6 7 8 9 10   026   99 98